T0157979

FOUR SCORE AND SEVEN BEERS AGO...

by
Brian T Shirley

Order this book online at www.trafford.com
or email orders@trafford.com

Most Trafford titles are also available at major online book retailers.

© Copyright 2011 Brian T Shirley.
All rights reserved. No part of this publication may be reproduced, stored in a retrieval system, or transmitted, in any form or by any means, electronic, mechanical, photocopying, recording, or otherwise, without the written prior permission of the author.

Author of " Make Love Not Warts".

Printed in the United States of America.

ISBN: 978-1-4269-7514-1 (sc)
ISBN: 978-1-4269-7515-8 (e)

Library of Congress Control Number: 2011911226

Trafford rev. 07/06/2011

 www.trafford.com

North America & international
toll-free: 1 888 232 4444 (USA & Canada)
phone: 250 383 6864 ✦ fax: 812 355 4082

Special Thanks and Credit:

Cover art done by Eric Grady

Edited by Sam Shirley

Special Thanks to the People, who supported, helped and contributed to this book:

Mom (Teresa Shirley) ,Grandma (Mary Hall), Sean,Lori,Brennon & Landon Shirley, Dad (Larry "Uncle Larry" Shirley), Sam Shirley, Robbie Ewen, Steve Hall, Radio Free " Rocky D", Scott Mann Wave 104.1, T&A morning show, Comedy Cabana, Spanky Brown, Dave Ugly(aka Dave Evans), Manny Olivera, Darryl Rhoades, Scott and Trish Adams, Tom and NONO, Eric Grady, Justin and Christy, Lisa, Tony Kemp, Warren Hicks, The Don Quixote Society, Bill Davis, Chris, Sandra & Jenny Merrill, Naughy, Fooboo and Gert PivPov. Greg Surette & Corg Pontell had nothing to do with this book.

They say happiness is on the inside;
I had mine surgically removed.

If it's a long way to Temporary,
it must take forever to get to Permanent.

It takes a village to raise an idiot.

I know into every life a little rain must fall,
but I feel like I should build an Ark!

If you don't laugh you'll cry,
but if you do both,
I'll laugh.

Blood is thicker than water,
especially if you get it from a turnip.

The more government cheese you get,
the more government cheese you want.

All roads lead to Rome, which is good because
I want some spaghetti.

Where ever you go you can't get rid of yourself...
unless you drink a lot.

Where there's a will, there are several greedy relatives.

Just when you think life couldn't suck anymore,
it blows!

Don't worry about putting the cart before the horse,
just use the tractor.

My Little China Girl says she's Turning Japanese,
so soon she'll be My Woman From Tokyo.

What does it profit a man if he has all the
rhythm in the world, yet no soul?

You can take a man out of the woods,
but then you have to give him welfare.

Only the "good" die young while the "evil" can't remember
where they parked their care.

My fan is totally covered, so what's the
shit going to hit next, my air conditioner?!

Two out of three ain't bad,
especially with runners in scoring position.

It's important to stay healthier than
your bank account.

I'm afraid of children because they're always swinging their
arms, which is right at crotch level.

"They " say you have to take the good with the bad,
I say we leave the bad with "they" and take off running.

You've Lost That Loving Feeling, meanwhile
I have become Comfortably Numb.

If happiness is a state of mind,
then sadness is a county in West Virginia.

There are honest politicians out there,
they just don't get elected.

George Washington had the toughest job as president,
because he couldn't blame the guy before him.

When life seems to be taking a dump on you,
hold your nose because there's probably more coming.

If we didn't have any problems in life,
then it would be all fun, and
that wouldn't be any fu..., hey, wait a minute!

Sometimes it's good to look older when you're young,
so as you age people will say
"Wow, you haven't changed!".

When you see someone get hurt,
don't ask them questions immediately,
give them a chance to adjust to their pain.

I'm so poor I drive a Ford Dilemma,
but at least it's an L.E.

Sex is a two-way street, unfortunately,
I feel as though I can't get out of the driveway.

Animals say the darndest things.

You're so full of crap, your eyes stink.

I was Taking Care Of Business at the Love Shack,
when I Fooled Around And Fell In Love.

I Twittered my Facebook, because I lost Myspace.

Don't nag people! Quit it! Your doing it again,
I told you not to NAG!!!

When life throws you a curve,
let it pass and wait for the fastball.

I've been called a "cracker",
but I prefer the term "saltine".

I'm all for fuel efficiency,
I just don't want to have to drive a plastic egg.

Don't pee on my leg then give me a weather forcast.

Who wants to sleep like a baby,
they don't stay down long and they always wake up cying.

If you keep looking at your watch during church,
what are you going to do when you get to Heaven?

If I were you, I'd be beside myself .

My dad told me I'd run into three assholes a day,
you've got me covered for the rest of the month!

I don't understand speed metal music.
If the song is so good, why are they in such
a hurry to get it over with?

Live free, die expensive.

Have you ever taken a vacation and then spent the
whole time worrying about how you can afford it?

People with egg on thier face have got to
stop rushing breakfast.

Yesterday is tomorrow's Grandpa.

They say a man thinks about sex once every thirty sec....,
damn, did you see the legs on her?

I don't mind getting older,
I just don't want other people to notice

If anyone asks you
"Could you be any more vague?",
just close your eyes and stand real still.

Sex sells, yet prostitution is illegal.

I can shake a stick at a lot of stuff.

It's good to be king, unless you're in San Francisco, then it's good to be queen.

Now your cooking with Earl!

To bury the hatchet, you need a shovel.

People are going to lie, I'm telling you the truth.

Middle age is great, because you can look back and
say, "What the hell was I thinking?", and
then look ahead and say "Oh crap!".

When you have to face the music,
make sure it's something you can sing along with.

Lola was Under Pressure,
so I told her to Relax, don't do it.

Sitting in traffic gives you a chance to
think of all the things you'd rather be doing.

It looks like another Low Fat Country Tuesday.

Never go to to bed angry, scream until you pass out.

Different strokes for different golfers.

How can I get you off my mind when
you won't get off my back.

Never burn your bridges, blow them up.

Cold hands, warm heart, red face.

Don't sweat the small stuff, sweat the hot stuff.

Make sure your trap is bigger than your bait!

You can put all your ducks in a row,
I'm going to scatter mine.

There's an elephant in the room and
he's wearing sunglasses and a plaid sweater.

If you learn from your mistakes,
then I must have a doctorate in stupidity.

You don't know what you have until it's gone,
which sucks,because you don't know what you're missing.

Don't put all your eggs in one basket,
you might want to hide some of them.

Teach a man to fish and he'll steal your pole.

One bad thing about the increase in life expectancy in
humans is that idiots now live longer.

Some people see the glass as half full, others see it as half empty,
meanwhile I don't even have a damn glass!

Give it all you've got, and if you don't succeed
you can always bitch about it later.

He who wins the war writes the history,
because who wants to listen to a loser.

You never know what's around the corner,
so I carry a stick with a mirror on it.

Out of the frying pan, onto the waistline.

If you can't beat'em, lick'em.

You Shook Me All Night Long,
so the next morning
I had Black Coffee In Bed.

Imitation is the slickest form of thievery.

When you make a mistake,
fake some sort of abdominal pain.

Don't throw the baby out with the bath water,
you'll get arrested.

You can fool some of the people some of the time, and
that's usually enough to do the trick.

My girlfriend broke up with me becasue she said she needed "to
find herself", so I suggested she get a GPS.

Even a fool can see an asshole in the distance.

You can only pluck a chicken once
before it's gets nervous.

The road is long and hard and so am I.

There's more than one way to skin a cat,
I just like using the same tool.

"One" is the loneliest number, while "one + a lawyer" is the most expensive.

Never trust someone who drives a car on a worn out donut.

Why be sad about the past when you can be sad about the present?

Let sleeping dogs lie, it's hard to tell the truth while your unconscious.

A fool and his money are soon parted,
and it usually involves a strip club.

Be careful of warning labels.

I walked around all day long with a banana in
my pocket smiling, and no one said a word to me.

I don't have an ego, but I do have an eggo.

Have you ever lost your mind and then
realized it was in your pants the whole time?

Self preservation to me is when I'm sitting in traffic and
I smell something oily or smokey, and I think to myself,
"Man, I hope that's someone else's car".

Mind your matter.

I've never killed two birds with one stone, but I did eat two
pieces of chicken once while I was stoned.

Speak once, think twice, wave three times.

I had Georgia On My Mind when someone started
talking about Sweet Home Alabama,
so I moved to Ohio.

I don't like dance songs that boss you around,
it reminds me of communism.

May you have a long night with a short hooker.

Read between the lies.

The grass isn't always greener on the other side,
sometimes the other side is a parking lot.   .

Head I win, tail I win.

Variety is the spice of life,
just don't use it
in your pudding.

I saw a Jewish porno movie once,
I guess you could say it was a neurotic movie.

Better a mud pie than mud pants.

Q) What kind of bus does an octopus drive?
A) An INK-U-BUS.(Incubus, stop it!)

You can put lipstick on a pig,
but it's still a.....hey, that's one hot looking sow!

Once a year go someplace you've never been and get someone else to pay for it.

Is there anything more ironic than an unemployed bill collector?

An ounce of preventiom is worth a ton of healthcare!

Don't cast pearls before swine, try corn.

The big difference between Rock music and Rap, is that rockers die from drugs and drinking, while rappers die from lead poisoning.

There's no "I" in "Team", but there is an "I" in "Win".

My dad is a scratch golfer, especially when the eraser on his pencil is worn down.

My mother didn't rinse our mouths out with soap, she used a brillo pad.

I like living in the past,
I was a lot younger and had more hair.

I Can't Drive 55 in my Little Red Corvette.

Reach for the stars, but watch out for that ceiling fan.

The grass is always greener if you get it from Canada.

When one door is shut,
someone locks it from the other side.

If the sale of hot cakes ever takes a dive,
our economy will be ruined.

Life isn't a dress rehearsal,
but you are free to change your costume.

I know I'm ahead of my time, because the
other day I woke up with my pants already on.

I'd rather wake up on the wrong side of the right bed,
than the right side of the wrong bed.

One world, one belly.

If I were twice as smart as I think you are,
I'd need to wear a helmet.

When the chips are down,
that means you won't need more dip.

Don't let people get under your skin, it will get infected.

It's nice to have friends,
because you can't complain to your enemies.

You can't always get what you want, and that really sucks!

Tomorrow will take care if itself,
that's why I'm calling in sick.

Take the road less traveled, there are no stop signs.

The poor shall inherit the earth,
as long as it's not within city limits.

Live everyday as if it's your last,
because one day it will be.

If there's a such thing as Global Warming,
it's caused by all the hot air coming from
people yelling about Global Warming!

Things aren't as bad as they seem, and
they smell a lot different than you think they will.

When someone gives you the cold shoulder,
put some of that "Icy/Hot" rubbing cream on it.

Marriage is a lot like football; when you're winning an
argument, just take a knee and don't run the score up.

Keep your feet clean, because you never know when
one will wind up in your mouth.

My mother didn't have eyes in the back of her head, but she did have a rearview mirror she carried with her at all times.

No matter how many times you paint a double-wide trailer, it can't cover up the appliances on the front porch.

I Can't Get No Satisfaction, Like A Virgin.

PETA gives me gas, and that's just cruel, just ask my family.

Don't mince words, mince meat!

Sometimes a kick in the ass is better than
a pat on the back, unless the kicker is using steel toed boots.

Children are best loved from afar.

Don't bite your hand.

I've learned that if you work your ass off,
you won't be able to sit down.

Man cannot live by bread alone, there's also wine.

You know you're driving slow when you
get passed by a hitchhiker.

When life has you by the balls, join a choir.

You're so perdy, oatmeal don't taste good no mo.

Late to bed, early to rise,
causes a man to
have red eyes.

I'll stop the world and Melt With You,
if you Pour Some Sugar On Me.

Why does Peter always get robbed and
Paul gets all the money?

I've seen a lot of commercials from lawyers that say they will fight for my rights, I want to know if that includes fighting for my right to PAARRRTTYY!!!

It's hard to look old when you're frolicking.

My finger stinks.

The early bird gets the morning wood.

This is the dawning of the Age of Aquariums.

If your testicles are removed and
afterwards all you do is sit and stare out at the backyard,
does that make you a window eunuch?

Pay attention when an old dog is barking,
he may not know where he is.

If you don't stand for something,
you'll be sitting down a lot.

I tried to kill someone with kindness once,
but all they did was thank me.

Don't complain about farmers with you mouth full,
they'll see you eating their food.

I'm a Renegade, Wanted Dead Or Alive,
so Gimme Back My Bullets.

Don't take life too seriously or it will kill you.

Don't worry about tomorrow until it's today,
then start crying.

Even Babe Ruth struck out sometimes, then
he sobered up and said, "What the hell happened?!".

If you put garbage in your head you'll be just like a trash can
and will have to run when you see the garbage truck coming.

Never say never. Damn it, I just said it twice.

Suround yourself with loving people,
but always use protection.

There are no pinch hitters in life,
but there's always someone warming up in the bullpen.

You can't change the past, but you can lie about it.

I had a Total Eclipse Of The Heart because
She Blinded Me With Science.

When someone calls you crazy,
tell them you'll think about it.

If you straddle the fence,
you'll wind up getting it in the end.

If happiness was a destination,
most people couldn't afford the air fare.

You know you're getting big when your ass is
considered carry on luggage.

You can't find answers at the bottom of a bottle,
just more questions like "Where did all the
stuff in the bottle go?".

Rome wasn't built in a day, you show me a city that was and
I'll show you poor infrastructure.

I had a girl break up with me because she said we had no
chemistry, so I told her I would become a scientist.

If it weren't for gossip,
how would we talk about each other?

Do naturalists ever dream they're on a
nude beach with all their clothes on?

All You Need Is Love and
Two Tickets To Paradies to Lay Down Sally.

If you dream you're taking a nap,
does that count as double the sleep?

Persistence is the key to....ah,I give up!

The further you lean to the left or the right polically,
the better chance you have of falling down.

A house divided, that's how I grew up.

A friend's eye is a good mirror,
especially if they wear glasses.

Something stinks in Denmark and
France isn't exactly a rose either.

A leopard can't change his spots,
but he can get some cool tattoos.

Money isn't everything...at lest
that's what I told my landlord.

We have two ears and one mouth for a reason,
and none of them must ever touch each other.

The shoe should never be on the other foot,
it shouldn't even fit.

A smile is a window into someone's heart,
unless your in Arkansas, then it's more like a fence.

When life gives you lemons, give life a rasberry.

Sometimes you're the road, sometimes you're on the
road crew holding that "slow" sign.

Even When Doves Cry, I Don't Stop Beleiving in this
Crazy Little Thing Called Love.

If you can't do something right the first time,
call a contractor.

Sometimes, depending on where you get it,
the short end of the stick can be a good thing.

Saying "Goodbye" isn't the hard part,
it's burying the body.

Revenge is a dish best served cold,
with a side of sinister laughter.

I have a monkey on my back and
he's throwing poop at everybody.

Be kind to people on the way up because one of
them may be bringing you your coffee.

It's alright for a grown man to cry as long as
he's cursing at the same time.

Another day, another dollar, another TAX!

Keeping it real is so tough,
because sometimes I feel so fake.

When a telemarketer calls, try to sell them your couch.

I don't want to go out with a "Bang!",
I want to go out with a blonde.

They say that if you don't love yourself, no one else will,
so I try to love myself as much as possible.

If you buy things you don't need,
then you are preparing for a yard sale.

Don't kick a man while he's down, sit on him.

You always hurt the ones you love.
That's why I punch my dad a lot.

Wish You Were Here at Our House so
we could put Another Brick In The Wall.

Don't ASK people to do something that
you are not willing to do, PAY them to do it.

It's never too late, unless her parents are home.

Beware of people with two faces,
it means someone married a cousin.

The squeaky wheel gets the early worm.

Fall seven times, man you're clumsy!

Whoever said "The pen is mightier than the sword", doesn't know a damn thing about fencing.

A lot of people walk in and out of your life, and some of them don't wipe thier shoes first.

Come On Eileen, let's go to Panama and drink some Red Wine while we're Sitting On The Dock Of The Bay.

When you go to a donkey's house don't talk about ears,
talk about the jackass next door.

There are plenty of fish in the sea,
unless you're an environmentalist.

Did you ever notice that ugly people
look older than they are?

No man can be an island unto himself,
unless he fills out the proper paperwork.

I've got a pet peeve, his name is Henry and
he eats a lot of sarcasm.

Two heads are better than one, but it looks weird.

The easiest way to double your money is to
fold it in half, put it in your pocket,
then throw your pants in a safe.

I did the Safety Dance with My Sharona while
Jessie's Girl Barked At The Moon.

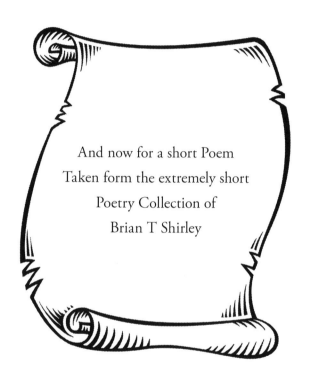

And now for a short Poem
Taken form the extremely short
Poetry Collection of
Brian T Shirley

The Bee

A flower's beauty is easy to see
as it's petals reach out like the branches of a tree
Gently try to pluck one and,...oops, there's a bee
"Ouch.., he stung me!"
"Damn Bee!!"

Thank You

Brian T Shirley is a professional comedian who has nearly twenty years in the business. He has performed all across the U.S., Canada, and The Bahamas. Born and raised in Marietta, GA., he now resides in Charleston, S.C.